# E A S Y   P I A N O
# SCOTT JOPLIN'S
## G R E A T E S T   H I T S

### ARRANGED BY CAROL KLOSE

| CONTENTS | | YEAR OF PUBLICATION |
|---|---|---|
| 4 | Bethena (A Concert Waltz) | 1905 |
| 8 | Bink's Waltz | 1905 |
| 12 | Crush Collision March | 1896 |
| 16 | Easy Winners, The (A Ragtime Two-Step) | 1901 |
| 24 | Entertainer, The (A Ragtime Two-Step) | 1902 |
| 28 | Eugenia | 1905 |
| 30 | Harmony Club Waltz | 1896 |
| 34 | Maple Leaf Rag | 1899 |
| 38 | Peacherine Rag | 1901 |
| 19 | Ragtime Dance ( A Stop-Time Two-Step) | 1906 |
| 41 | Solace (A Mexican Serenade) | 1909 |
| 44 | Swipesy | 1900 |

### HAL•LEONARD®
### CORPORATION
7777 W. BLUEMOUND RD. P.O. BOX 13819 MILWAUKEE, WI 53213

ISBN 978-0-7935-0577-7

Copyright © 1991 by HAL LEONARD PUBLISHING CORPORATION
International Copyright Secured   All Rights Reserved

For all works contained herein:
Unauthorized copying, arranging, adapting, recording or public performance is an infringement of copyright.
Infringers are liable under the law.

# INTRODUCTION

This book, "Scott Joplin's Greatest Hits," is a collection of the best-known Joplin compositions, arranged for Easy Piano. These songs include not only rags, but compositions in other styles as well: lyrical waltzes, an exciting march, and a Mexican serenade. While the selections have been shortened and simplified to accommodate the easy piano level, every effort has been made to preserve the feeling of the original music. This volume makes it possible for even the inexperienced pianist to enjoy recreating the sounds of the "King of Ragtime."

## SCOTT JOPLIN

Born in Texarkana, Texas in 1868, Scott Joplin came from a musical family of six children. His father, an ex-slave, played violin, while his mother sang and played the banjo. At an early age young Scott was playing piano and improvising well beyond his years. Soon he was given formal lessons in piano, sight-reading and basic harmony.

In 1882, at the age of fourteen, Joplin moved from home and began playing in honky-tonk establishments from Louisiana up through the Mississipi Valley states - the very area that saw the birth of ragtime.

In his travels over the next three years Joplin was exposed to the wide variety of music that was being played or sung by both blacks and whites at the time: folk songs, light classical music, original compositions, popular music. Out of this melting pot would emerge the musical style known as ragtime, and Scott Joplin would soon become the master of the ragtime generation.

By 1885 Joplin settled, more or less, in St. Louis, where he had the opportunity to observe the many styles of music that abounded in that center of steamboat traffic and river trade. In 1893 he performed in the ragtime district of Chicago during the Chicago World's Fair, allowing him time to mingle with influential musicians who gathered there from throughout the country.

After 1893 he continued to move between St. Louis and Sedalia, Missouri, becoming an integral part of the ragtime scene wherever he went. He formed the Texas Medley Quartette, traveling as far as New York State, and began composing vocal songs and piano solos. In 1895 he sold his first pieces for publication, and by 1897 had written his most famous work, the "Maple Leaf Rag" (published two years later).

By 1896, his wanderings basically over, Joplin settled down in Sedalia where he took courses in harmony and composition at a local college and became the central figure of the area's black musical scene. In that same year, the introduction of ragtime to a New York stage audience caused a national sensation, paving the way for publication of ragtime songs. Through sheet music, ragtime would now be preserved and made accessible to every household in America.

The publication of the "Maple Leaf Rag" in 1899 launched Scott Joplin as the "King Of Ragtime." His popularity increased with the publication of more great hits, such as "The Easy Winners" (1901), "The Entertainer" (1902), and "Bethena" (1905).

In 1907 Joplin moved to New York City, where he was able to live off his royalties and spend more time teaching and composing. There, in 1917, despondent over the failure of his folk opera "Treemonisha" and suffering from rapidly deteriorating health, Scott Joplin died at the age of forty-nine.

Today the music of Scott Joplin remains as fresh and enjoyable as when it was first written - proof of the great legacy of this immortal American composer.

# PLAYING THE MUSIC OF SCOTT JOPLIN WITH EASE

## SYNCOPATION

One characteristic of the music of Scott Joplin is syncopation - the shift of the rhythmic accent from a strong beat to a weak beat.  This "new" feature of popular music at the turn of the century was such an important part of Joplin's compositions that he published a series of exercises called "School Of Ragtime" to help pianists play his syncopated ragtime rhythms more easily.

In the following example, simplified from the original version in "School Of Ragtime", you will see how Joplin presented syncopation in a step-by-step way.

If you are new to ragtime rhythm, try playing this example both ways: first the "straight" version (A), then the syncopated version (B).  Add the left-hand part (lowest staff) each time.

Before many of the arrangements in this book you will see one or two short rhythm exercises like the one below that introduce the syncopated rhythm patterns featured in that particular song.

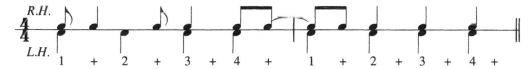

Before playing the song, try tapping each exercise a few times on a table top or on your knees.  Use your right hand to tap notes with stems up, and your left hand to tap notes with stems down.  Repeat the exercise several times.  Tap slowly at first, and gradually increase your speed until the rhythm of the two hands becomes second nature to you.

## PLAYING TIPS:

1.  Check for sharps or flats in the key signature before you begin.
2.  Try to play without looking at the keys or your hands.
3.  Follow the fingering suggestions shown in the music.
4.  Play the right-hand and left-hand parts separately a few times before playing the song "hands together."
5.  Check the song for repeats, D.S. signs, Codas, etc., before you begin.
6.  As you become more and more familiar with the song, relax and have fun!

Practice Rhythm:

# BETHENA
## (A CONCERT WALTZ)

By SCOTT JOPLIN

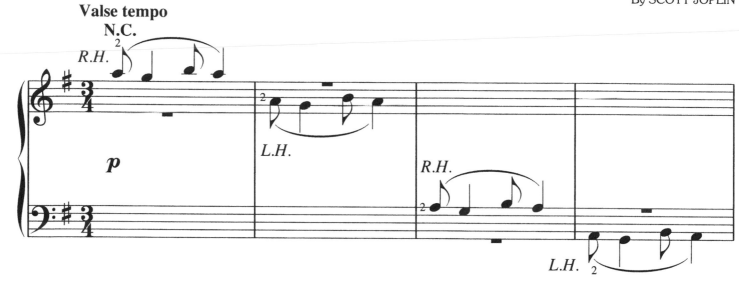

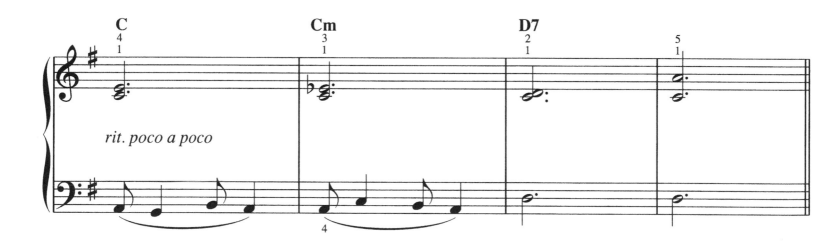

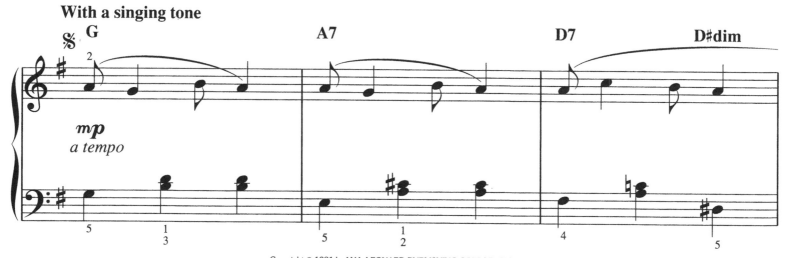

Copyright © 1991 by HAL LEONARD PUBLISHING CORPORATION
International Copyright Secured   All Rights Reserved

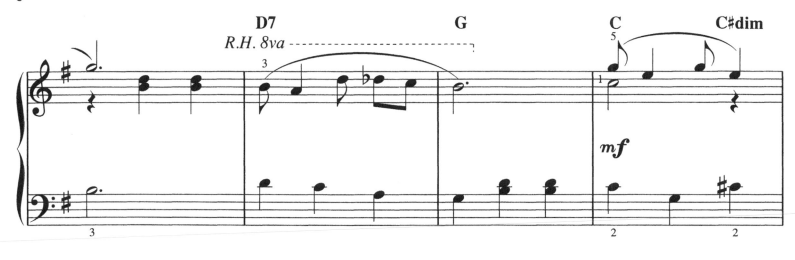

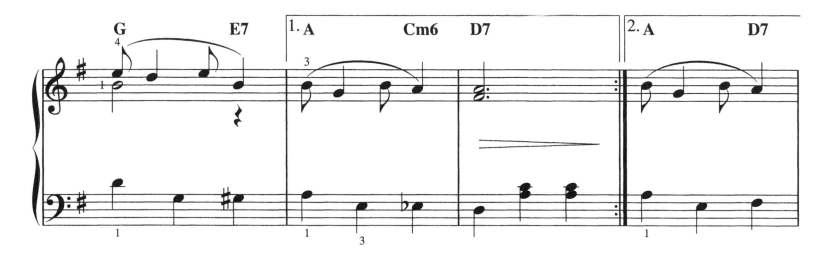

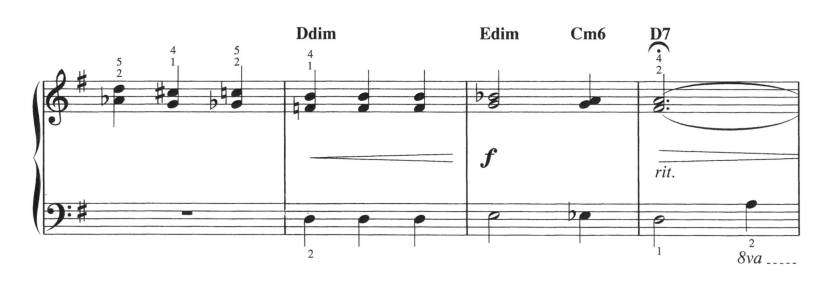

# BINK'S WALTZ

By SCOTT JOPLIN

**Expressive waltz tempo**

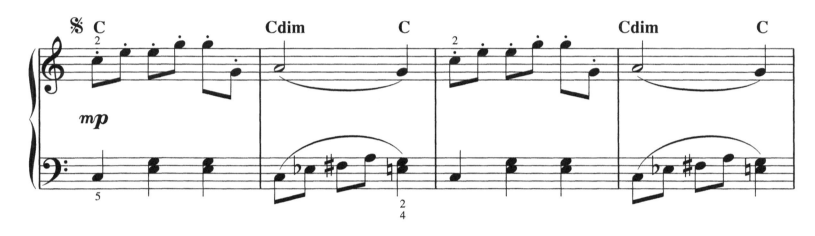

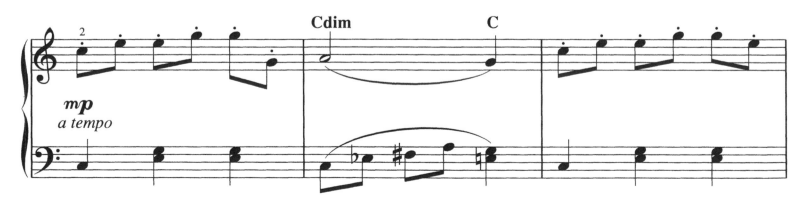

Copyright © 1991 by HAL LEONARD PUBLISHING CORPORATION
International Copyright Secured    All Rights Reserved

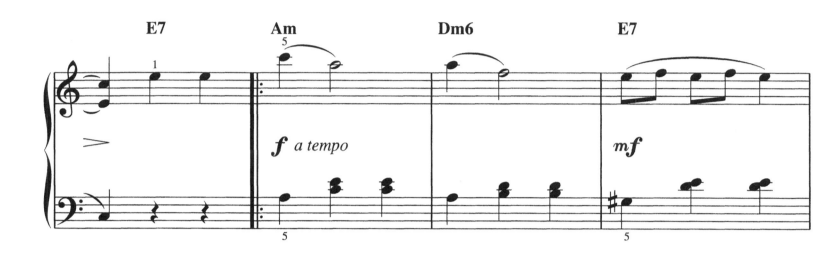

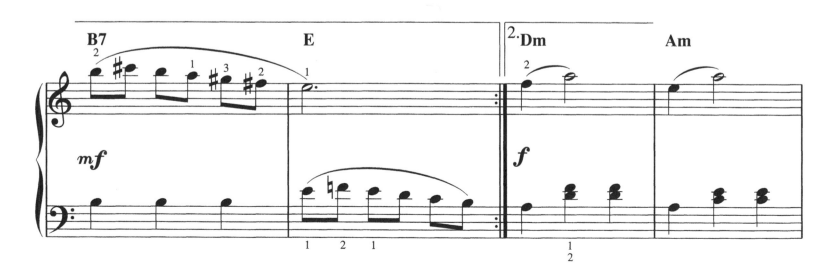

# CRUSH COLLISION MARCH

By SCOTT JOPLIN

Copyright © 1991 by HAL LEONARD PUBLISHING CORPORATION
International Copyright Secured   All Rights Reserved

14

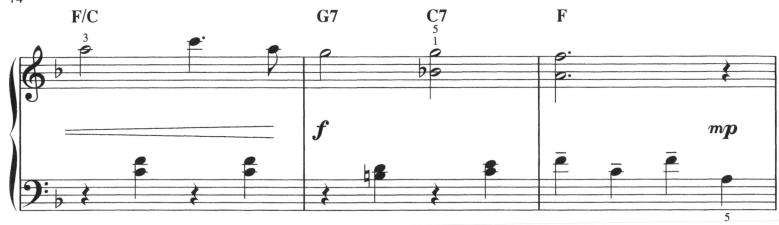

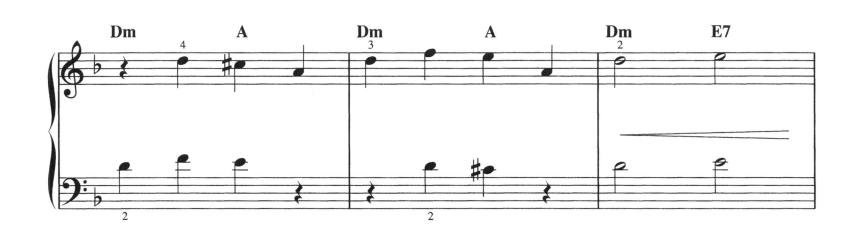

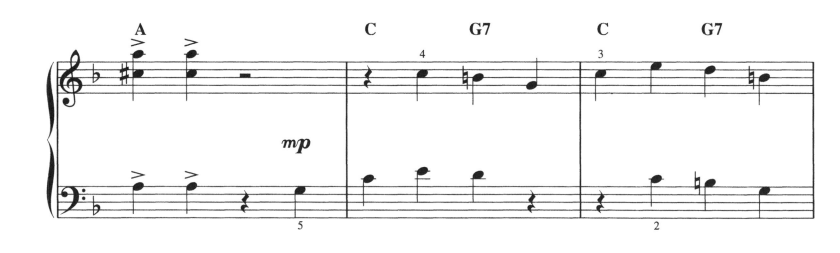

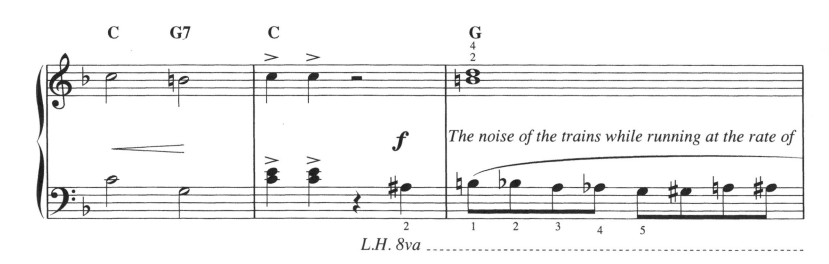

*The noise of the trains while running at the rate of*

L.H. 8va - - - - - - - - - - - - - - - - - - - - - - - - - - - - - - - - - - - - - - - - - - - - - - - - -

sixty miles per hour

Whistling for the crossing

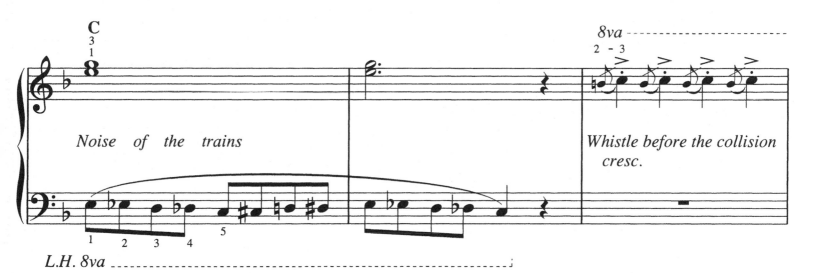

Noise of the trains

Whistle before the collision
*cresc.*

*L.H. 8va*

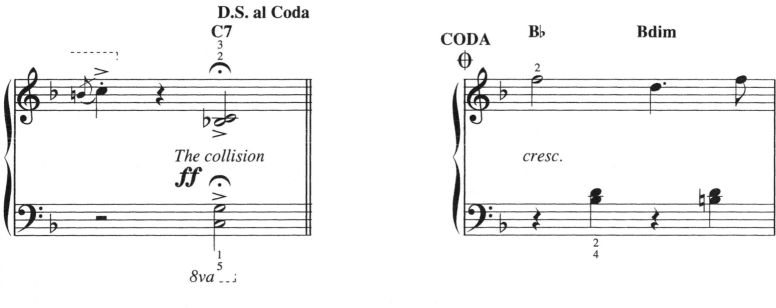

**D.S. al Coda**

C7

*The collision*
**ff**

**CODA**

B♭

Bdim

*cresc.*

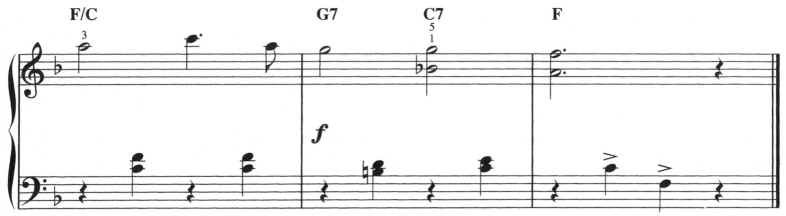

F/C

G7

C7

F

*f*

Practice Rhythm A.

Practice Rhythm B.

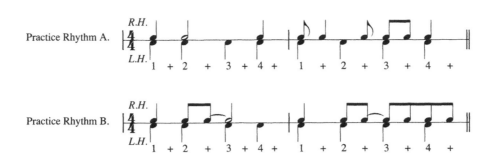

# THE EASY WINNERS
## (A RAGTIME TWO-STEP)

By SCOTT JOPLIN

**Easy march feel**

*L.H. detached throughout*

Copyright © 1991 by HAL LEONARD PUBLISHING CORPORATION
International Copyright Secured   All Rights Reserved

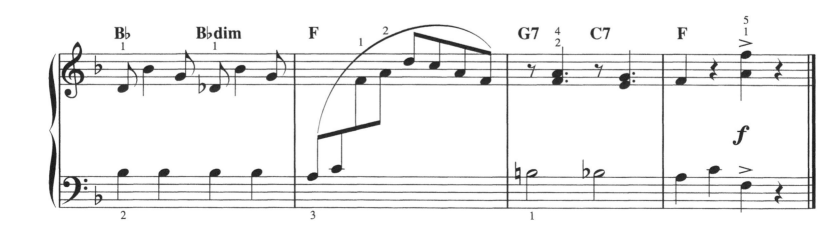

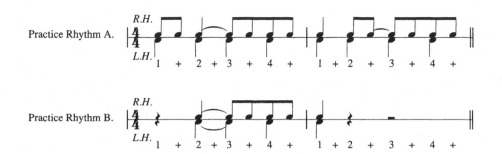

# RAGTIME DANCE
## (A STOP-TIME TWO-STEP)

By SCOTT JOPLIN

Copyright © 1991 by HAL LEONARD PUBLISHING CORPORATION
International Copyright Secured   All Rights Reserved

* Joplin's directions:  "NOTICE:  To get the desired effect of 'Stop Time',  the pianist will please Stamp the heel of one
foot heavily upon the floor at the word 'Stamp.'  Do not raise the toe from the floor while "stamping."
(Instead of "stamping", a second person can "clap" the "stamp" rhythm along with the pianist.)

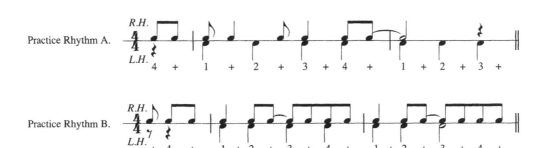

# THE ENTERTAINER
## (A RAG-TIME TWO-STEP)

By SCOTT JOPLIN

**Not fast**

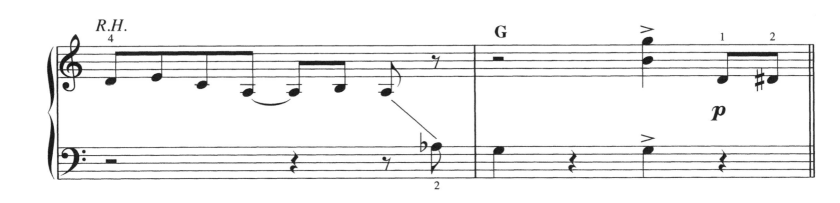

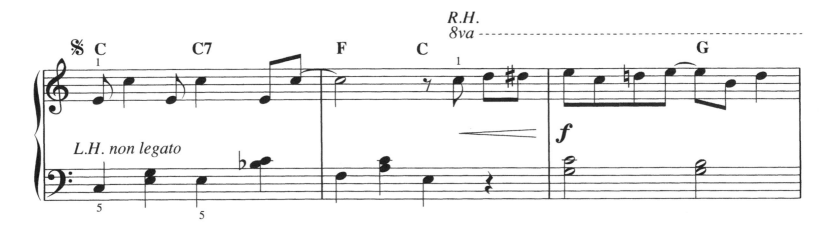

Copyright © 1991 by HAL LEONARD PUBLISHING CORPORATION
International Copyright Secured    All Rights Reserved

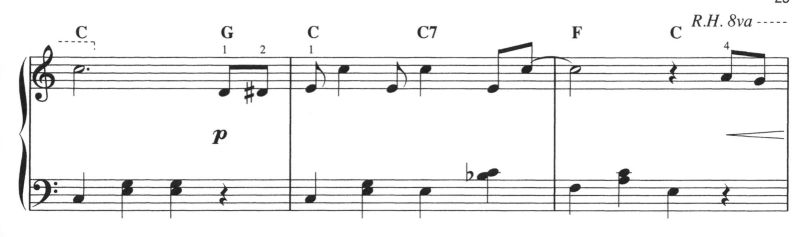

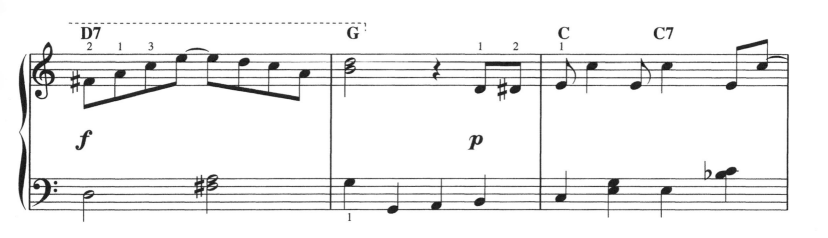

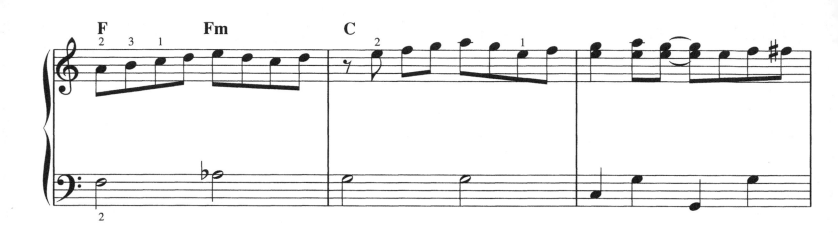

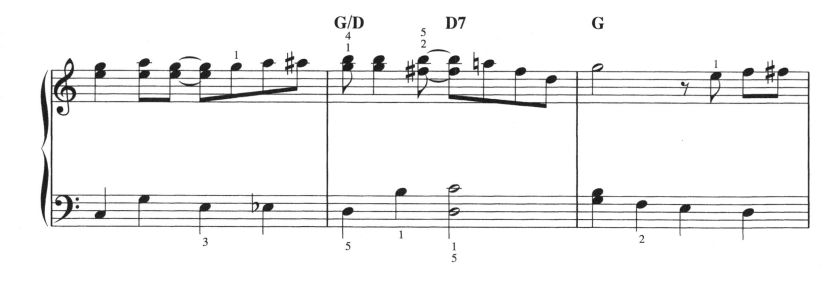

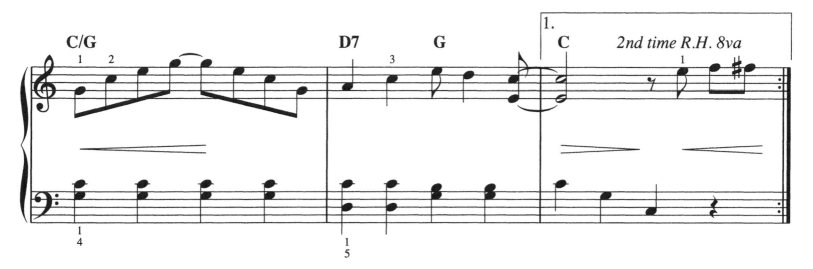

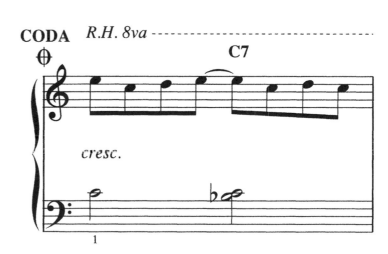

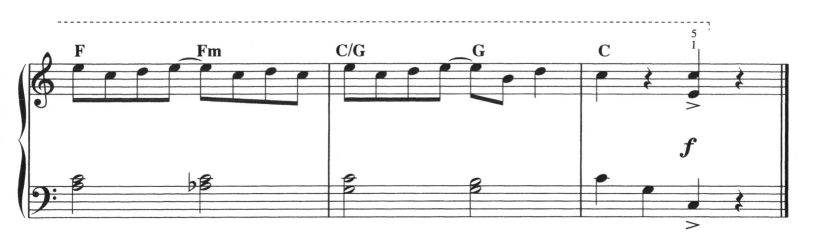

Practice Rhythm:

# EUGENIA

By SCOTT JOPLIN

**Slow march tempo**

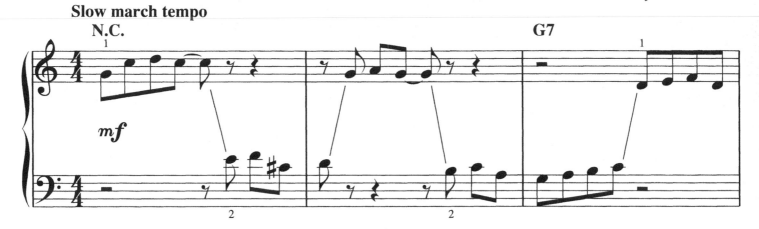

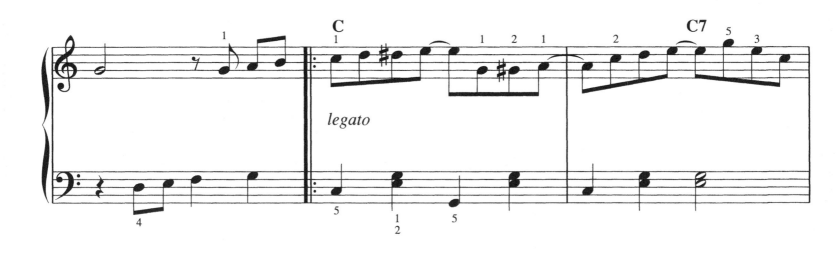

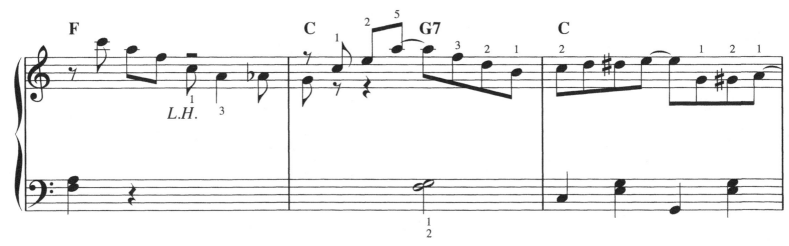

Copyright © 1991 by HAL LEONARD PUBLISHING CORPORATION
International Copyright Secured    All Rights Reserved

# HARMONY CLUB WALTZ

By SCOTT JOPLIN

Copyright © 1991 by HAL LEONARD PUBLISHING CORPORATION
International Copyright Secured   All Rights Reserved

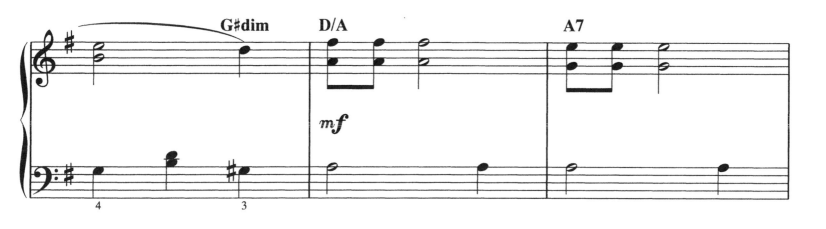

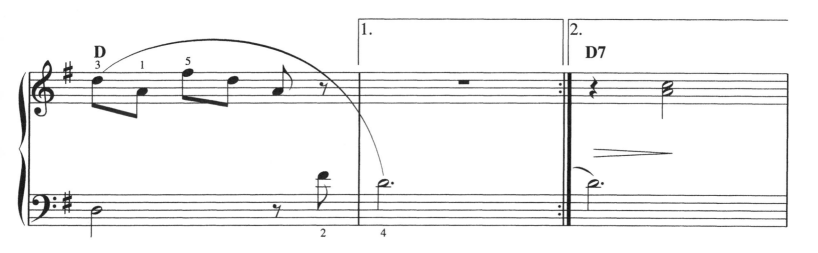

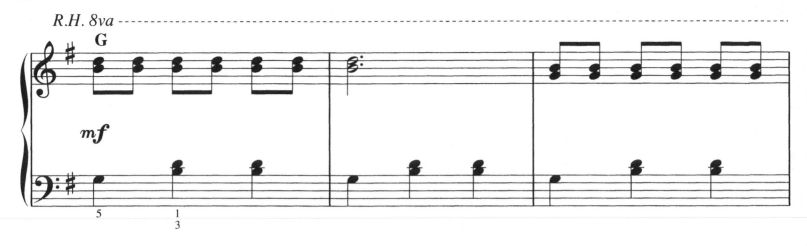

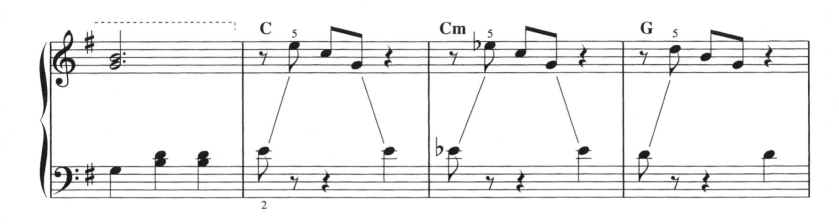

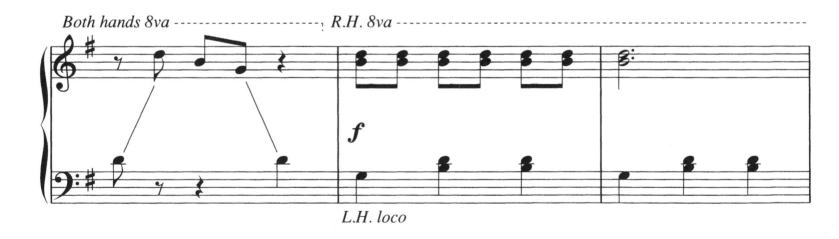

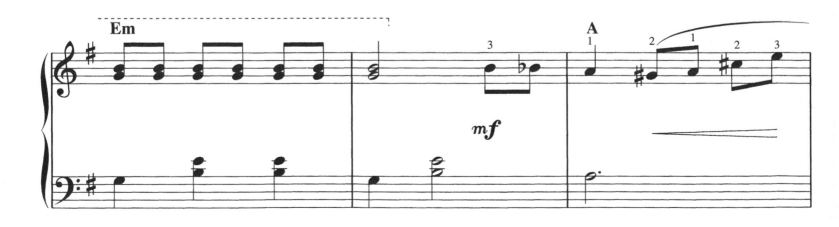

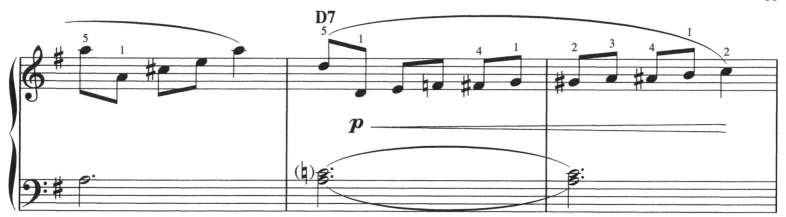

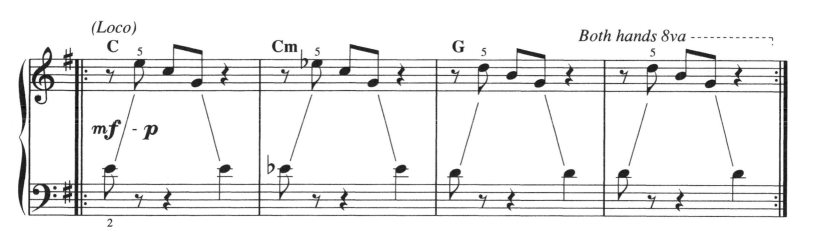

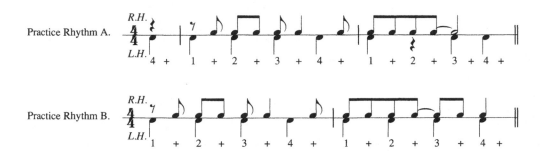

Practice Rhythm A.

Practice Rhythm B.

# MAPLE LEAF RAG

By SCOTT JOPLIN

**With a deliberate march feel**

*L.H. play in a detached manner throughout*

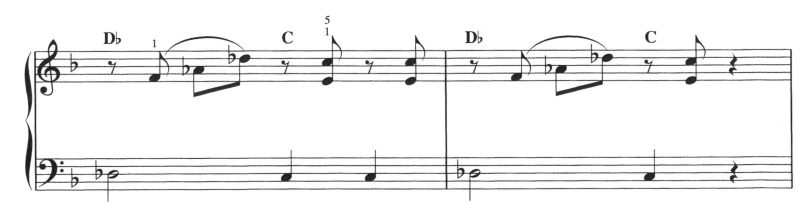

Copyright © 1991 by HAL LEONARD PUBLISHING CORPORATION
International Copyright Secured   All Rights Reserved

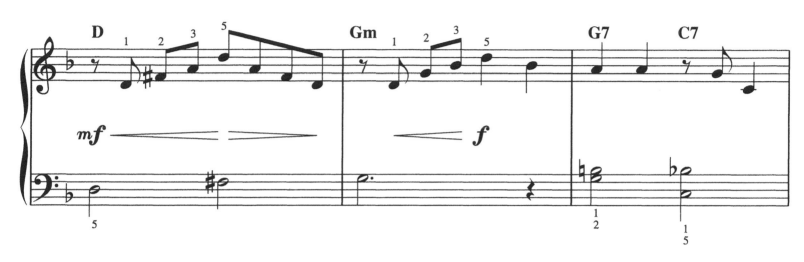

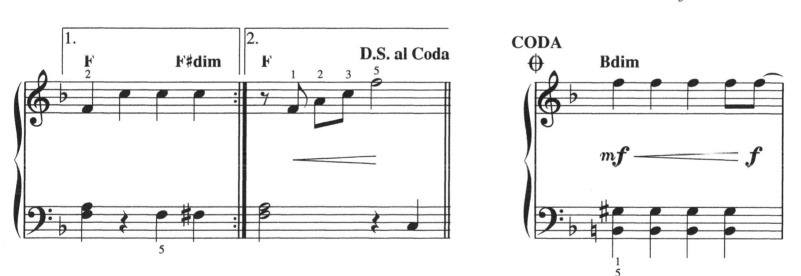

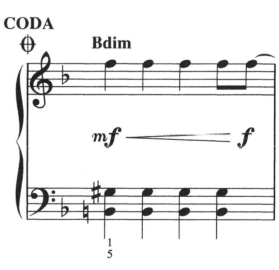

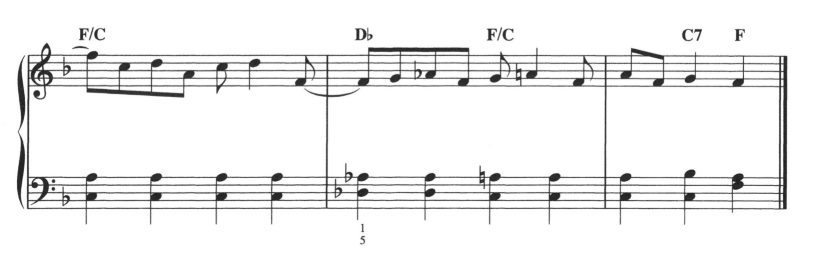

Practice Rhythm A.

Practice Rhythm B.

# PEACHERINE RAG

By SCOTT JOPLIN

**Not too fast**

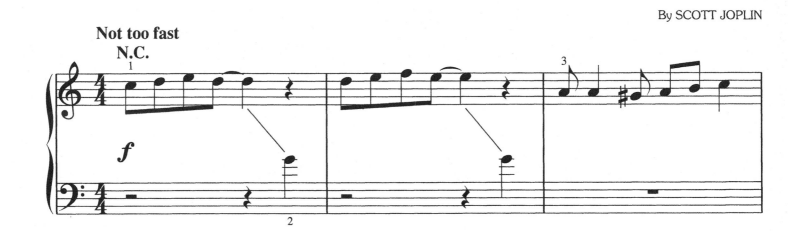

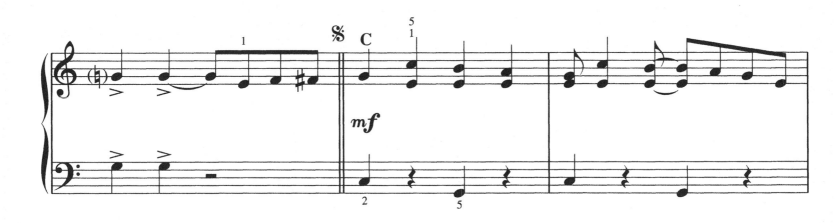

Copyright © 1991 by HAL LEONARD PUBLISHING CORPORATION
International Copyright Secured   All Rights Reserved

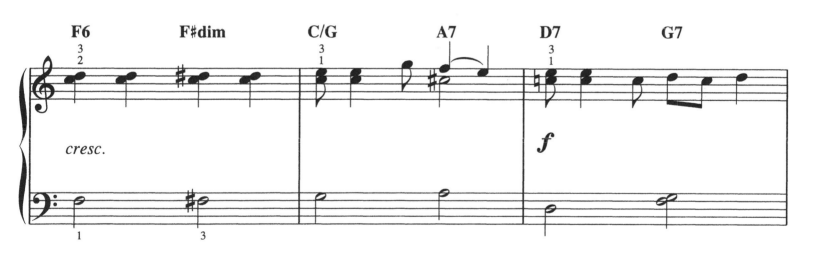

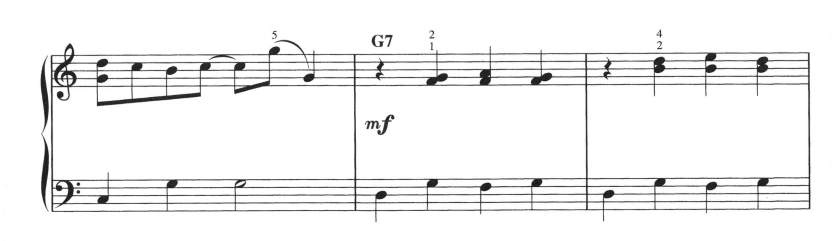

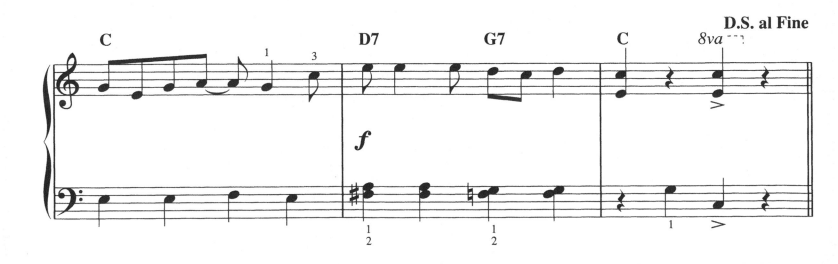

Practice Rhythm A.

Practice Rhythm B.

# SOLACE
## (A MEXICAN SERENADE)

By SCOTT JOPLIN

Very slow march time

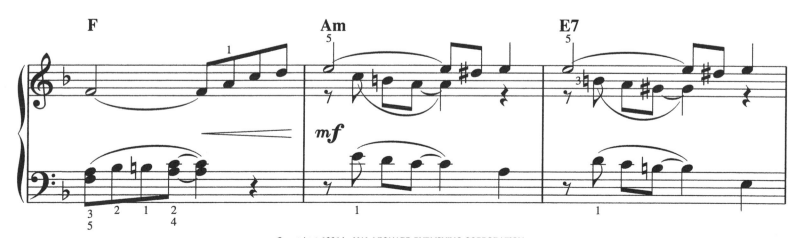

Copyright © 1991 by HAL LEONARD PUBLISHING CORPORATION
International Copyright Secured   All Rights Reserved

# SWIPESY
## (CAKE WALK)

By SCOTT JOPLIN
and ARTHUR MARSHALL

**Slow march tempo**

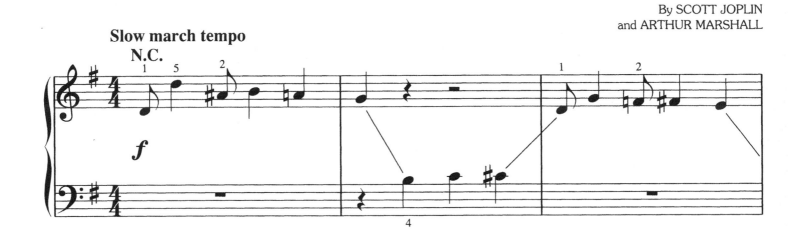

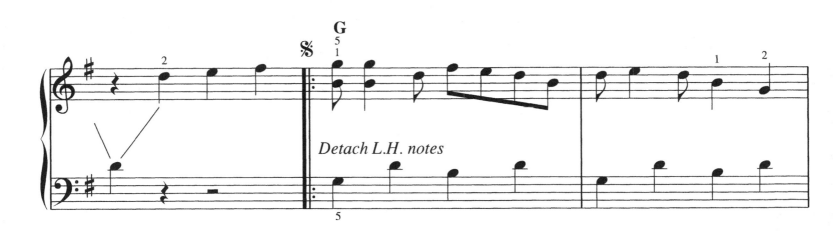

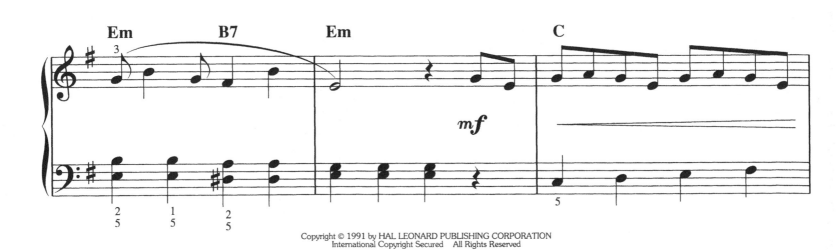

Copyright © 1991 by HAL LEONARD PUBLISHING CORPORATION
International Copyright Secured   All Rights Reserved

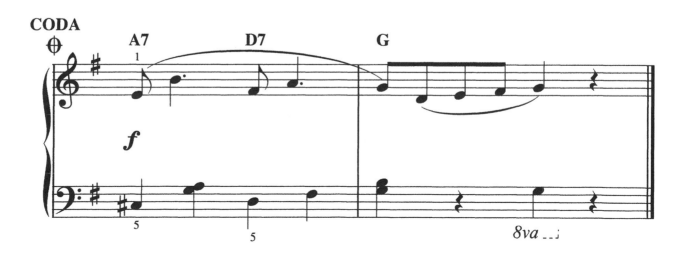

# YOUR FAVORITE MUSIC
# ARRANGED FOR PIANO SOLO

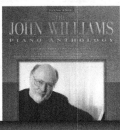

## ARTIST, COMPOSER, TV & MOVIE SONGBOOKS

**Adele for Piano Solo**
00307585.....................$17.99

**The Beatles Piano Solo**
00294023.....................$17.99

**A Charlie Brown Christmas**
00313176.....................$17.99

**Paul Cardall – The Hymns Collection**
00295925.....................$24.99

**Coldplay for Piano Solo**
00307637.....................$17.99

**Selections from Final Fantasy**
00148699.....................$19.99

**Alexis Ffrench – The Sheet Music Collection**
00345258.....................$19.99

**Game of Thrones**
00199166.....................$17.99

**Hamilton**
00345612.....................$19.99

**Hillsong Worship Favorites**
00303164.....................$12.99

**How to Train Your Dragon**
00138210.....................$19.99

**Elton John Collection**
00306040.....................$22.99

**La La Land**
00283691.....................$14.99

**John Legend Collection**
00233195.....................$17.99

**Les Misérables**
00290271.....................$19.99

**Little Women**
00338470.....................$19.99

**Outlander: The Series**
00254460.....................$19.99

**The Peanuts® Illustrated Songbook**
00313178.....................$24.99

**Astor Piazzolla – Piano Collection**
00285510.....................$17.99

**Pirates of the Caribbean – Curse of the Black Pearl**
00313256.....................$19.99

**Pride & Prejudice**
00123854.....................$17.99

**Queen**
00289784.....................$19.99

**John Williams Anthology**
00194555.....................$24.99

**George Winston Piano Solos**
00306822.....................$22.99

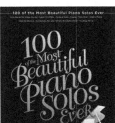
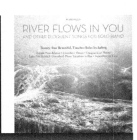

## MIXED COLLECTIONS

**Beautiful Piano Instrumentals**
00149926.....................$16.99

**Best Jazz Piano Solos Ever**
00312079.....................$24.99

**Best Piano Solos Ever**
00242928.....................$19.99

**Big Book of Classical Music**
00310508.....................$19.99

**Big Book of Ragtime Piano**
00311749.....................$22.99

**Christmas Medleys**
00350572.....................$16.99

**Disney Medleys**
00242588.....................$17.99

**Disney Piano Solos**
00313128.....................$17.99

**Favorite Pop Piano Solos**
00312523.....................$16.99

**Great Piano Solos**
00311273.....................$16.99

**The Greatest Video Game Music**
00201767.....................$19.99

**Most Relaxing Songs**
00233879.....................$17.99

**Movie Themes Budget Book**
00289137.....................$14.99

**100 of the Most Beautiful Piano Solos Ever**
00102787.....................$29.99

**100 Movie Songs**
00102804.....................$29.99

**Peaceful Piano Solos**
00286009.....................$17.99

**Piano Solos for All Occasions**
00310964.....................$24.99

**River Flows in You & Other Eloquent Songs**
00123854.....................$17.99

**Sunday Solos for Piano**
00311272.....................$17.99

**Top Hits for Piano Solo**
00294635.....................$14.99

View songlists online and order from your favorite music retailer at
**halleonard.com**

*Prices, content, and availability subject to change without notice.*

Disney characters and artwork TM & © 2021 Disney

0621
195